Earn Money From Home

Allison Evans

Copyright Page

First edition

Index

The Freedom of Living from Home

The freedom of living from home is a concept that many long for, but few truly understand until they experience it. It's about more than just working in your pajamas or avoiding the morning traffic. It's a complete transformation in the way you live, organize your time, and perceive the world. Living from home while earning an income is a gateway to a lifestyle where you are in control — not your boss, not an office, not a schedule that doesn't suit you.

Imagine waking up every morning without the pressure of an alarm clock forcing you to rush out the door. Instead of a long commute on public transport or in a car, you start your day with a leisurely breakfast, perhaps accompanied by some time for yourself - reading, meditating or simply enjoying the silence. This small change in routine has a huge impact. It allows you to start the day calmly and in control, something that rarely happens when you rely on a traditional job outside the home.

Freedom isn't just physical, it's mental too. By working from home, you leave behind many of the stresses that come with an office environment: the endless meetings, the workplace politics, the constant supervision. At home, you decide how to organize your day. If you want to work intensively in the morning and enjoy a free afternoon, you do that. If you prefer to divide your tasks into small blocks so you have frequent breaks, that's possible too. This level of flexibility is unthinkable for most people stuck in rigid schedules.

However, the true essence of living from home is not just about work. It's about life itself. By not wasting hours of your day commuting, you can invest that time in what really matters: spending more time with your family, taking care of your health, learning something new, or even developing personal projects that you always put aside due to lack of time. Earning money from home is not just a way of working, it's a lifestyle that allows you to align your income with your personal values and priorities.

Another key aspect of this freedom is that you are not limited by a geographic location. If one day you decide that you prefer to work from a cabin in the woods, a quiet beach, or even in another country, you can do so. Your office is not a physical location, but rather an internet connection and your skills. This type of freedom, once a luxury reserved for a select few, is now possible for anyone willing to adapt and learn.

Of course, freedom also comes with responsibilities. Living from home requires discipline. There’s no one telling you what to do or when to do it. You’re the one who has to set your goals, stay focused, and make sure your income flows in. But this autonomy is what makes it all worthwhile. Instead of working to fulfill someone else’s dreams, you’re building your own.

Making money from home is more than a change in how you work; it's a change in how you live. With each passing day, you realize that you don't need to wait until you're 60 or 65 to enjoy "retirement." You can enjoy your life now, while generating income and staying productive. This lifestyle doesn't mean working less, but working better, with purpose and on your own terms.

The freedom of living from home isn't about escaping responsibilities, but about taking them on in a smarter way. It's about designing your life in a way that makes you feel fulfilled, free, and in control. If you've ever felt like the traditional way of working doesn't fit you, this is your chance to prove that there is another way to live. And it's not only possible, it's deeply rewarding.

Is it Really Possible to Retire Early?

Retiring early is an idea that sounds like an impossible dream to many people, but the reality is that it is not only possible, but it is within reach of those who understand how money works and how to design a different life. Early retirement does not mean stopping work completely, but rather achieving the freedom to choose if you want to work, how to do it and for what. It is a concept that breaks with the traditional idea of waiting until 60 or 65 years old to start enjoying life.

To understand this, we must first talk about what a "pension" means. In the classical sense, it is an income that you receive after years of work, usually from an employer or the government. But in the context of retiring early, the pension does not come from a traditional system, but from income that you yourself generate through independent sources. These can be investments, businesses, home-based jobs, or passive income that allows you to cover your expenses without depending on a fixed schedule or a specific location.

So how is it possible to achieve this goal? The first step is to change the way we view money. Many people spend their lives working to earn money, but they never stop to think about how to make that money work for them. Here’s the secret. When you start investing in things that generate income, such as property, stocks, digital businesses, or even your knowledge, you are getting closer to early retirement. Every dollar you invest becomes a silent worker that keeps generating more money for you, even when you are not actively working.

Another important aspect is cutting down on unnecessary expenses. It's not about living like a monk, but rather prioritizing what really matters. Many times, we spend money on things we don't need simply because we're stressed or because we want to impress others. If you eliminate those expenses and use that money to create sources of income, you're paving your way to a freer life.

Working from home is one of the most effective strategies for moving towards early retirement. This work model eliminates costs such as commuting, office clothes, or eating out. But beyond saving, it allows you to have time to develop projects that generate additional income. For example, you could dedicate part of your day to learning about investments, creating an online business, or selling your skills as a freelancer. These types of activities are the bridge that leads you to financial independence.

Once your passive income covers your monthly expenses, you can consider yourself "retired," even if you continue to work at what you love. The difference is that you no longer work out of necessity, but out of choice. This is the true meaning of retiring early: having the freedom to decide how you want to live your life without money being a constant concern.

Of course, it's not something that happens overnight. It requires planning, effort, and above all, a different mindset. You need to be consistent, willing to learn, and in some cases, take calculated risks. But every small step you take in this direction brings you closer to a life free of financial stress.

It's important to note that early retirement doesn't mean you'll stop being productive. Many people who achieve this lifestyle find that they have more energy and creativity to pursue projects they're truly passionate about. They can start their own business, help others, or even travel the world while working on something they find fulfilling. The difference is that they no longer rely on a biweekly paycheck to survive.

So yes, it is possible to retire early. It's not a fantasy reserved for a select few, but an attainable goal for those willing to step outside the traditional mindset. You don't have to wait decades to enjoy life. With the right strategies and a clear focus, you can start building your financial freedom today. The road won't always be easy, but each step will lead you toward a life where time and money work for you, not against you. And that, without a doubt, is a life worth living.

The Financial Independence Mindset

A financial independence mindset is the first step to achieving the freedom that many desire, but few achieve. It is much more than having money in the bank or earning a good salary. It is a way of thinking and acting that allows you to take control of your finances and design a life that does not depend on a steady job, a boss or a stable economy. Having this mindset means that you decide how to generate income, how to spend it and how to make it work for you, instead of being a slave to money.

The first shift you need to make in your mindset is to stop thinking of money as an end and start seeing it as a tool. Many people spend their lives working hard to earn money, but they immediately spend it on things that don't provide them with long-term value. The financial independence mindset teaches you to use money to build a system that makes more money. It's not about how much you make, but how you use what you have.

One of the keys to this mindset is understanding the difference between assets and liabilities. Assets are things that put money in your pocket, such as investments, businesses, properties, or income-generating projects. Liabilities, on the other hand, are things that take money out of your pocket, such as debt, unnecessary expenses, or assets that do not generate value. Financial independence is achieved by accumulating assets that work for you. This doesn't mean you should live like a cheapskate, but it does mean you should learn to prioritize what really matters.

Another essential aspect of this mindset is breaking away from the fear of risk. Many people avoid investing or starting a project for fear of losing money. But the reality is that the real risk is in doing nothing. If you continue to rely on a single income, such as a salary, you are in a fragile situation. The world is constantly changing, and what is safe today might not be tomorrow. The mindset of financial independence involves accepting that some risks are necessary, as long as they are calculated and you have a plan.

Discipline also plays a key role. Living financially independent isn't a stroke of luck, it's the result of consistent decisions over time. This means learning to say no to certain expenses, sticking to a budget, and being consistent in your efforts to generate additional income. Often, people who appear to have financial freedom have simply been more disciplined with their money and time than others.

Patience is another pillar of this mindset. Often, the rewards don't come right away. Building assets and having them generate income takes time, but it's a cumulative process. Every small action you take today, like saving, investing, or learning a new skill, brings you closer to financial independence. It's like planting a tree: you don't see much progress at first, but over time, the fruits are inevitable.

Financial independence also requires surrounding yourself with the right mindset. This means learning from people who have already achieved what you want. Read books, listen to podcasts, seek out mentors. Avoid the opinions of those who only see problems and not solutions. If you constantly listen to people who say that financial freedom is impossible, it will be harder to believe in yourself. Surround yourself with examples that inspire you and keep you focused.

Finally, having this mindset means redefining what success means to you. It's not about having more money than others or buying things to impress. It's about creating a life that makes you happy, where money is not a constant concern and where you can dedicate your time to what really matters: your family, your dreams, your health and your well-being. Financial independence is not just a goal, it's a way to live in balance, without depending on anyone else for security and peace of mind.

Developing this mindset doesn't happen overnight, but every step you take toward it will make a difference. Start by learning, changing your habits, and making conscious choices about how you use your time and money. Little by little, you'll realize that you don't need to follow the traditional path to live the life you want. Financial freedom starts in your mind, and everything else follows after.

Your Office, Your World

Your office, your world, is more than just a nice phrase. It’s an idea that transforms the way you work and live. When you work from home, you have the power to create a space that is not only functional, but reflects who you are and what you want to accomplish. You are no longer limited by grey cubicles and impersonal desks. Your office can be a place that inspires you, motivates you, and most importantly, makes you feel comfortable.

The first step to building your world at home is to understand that your office is much more than a desk and a chair. It's the place where your dreams will happen. That's why you need to design it with intention. Think about what makes you feel good. Maybe it's a window with a nice view, some plants that bring life to the space, or just a clean and organized desk. This isn't just a place to work, it's the heart of your productivity.

One important thing is to choose a place in your home that is exclusively for work. It doesn't have to be an entire room; it can be a corner in the living room or a table in your bedroom. The important thing is that it is yours and that you associate it with your professional activity. When you have a defined space, it is easier to concentrate and separate work from the rest of your life. This also helps the people you live with understand that when you are in your office, you are in "work mode."

Comfort is key. You'll be spending many hours at your desk, so invest in a good chair that supports your posture and a desk that's the right size for your needs. If you work at a computer, make sure it's at the right height to avoid neck or back pain. These details may seem small, but they make a big difference in your energy and productivity throughout the day.

Lighting is another aspect that you shouldn't overlook. A well-lit office not only improves your mood, but also your efficiency. If possible, place your desk near a window to take advantage of natural light. If you don't have that option, invest in a lamp that illuminates your workspace well. A warm, pleasant light can make long hours in front of a screen much more bearable.

Also, your office should reflect your personality. This is where the magic of making it your world comes in. Decorate your space with things that inspire you: photos of happy moments, a motivational quote, your favorite books, or even little things that make you smile. This is your territory, and you should feel happy being there. But remember, don't overload the space. A clean and tidy environment will always be more productive than one filled with distractions.

Technology also plays a big role. Make sure you have a reliable internet connection, well-functioning devices, and everything you need to get your work done without interruptions. Nothing slows down productivity more than constantly dealing with technical issues. If you need specific tools, such as software or additional equipment, consider it an investment in your success. This is your business and your future.

It's also important to set boundaries. Your office may be at home, but that doesn't mean you're always available. Set clear work hours and stick to them. Let your family or roommates know about those times so they respect your space and time. Learning to switch off when your workday is over is key to maintaining a balance between your personal and professional life.

Finally, remember that your office doesn't have to be a static place. If you ever feel bored or need a change, you can rearrange the furniture, change the decor, or even move your workspace to another part of the house. Flexibility is one of the biggest advantages of working from home, and your office can adapt to your needs and emotions.

Your office, your world, is exactly that: your space to create, grow and achieve your goals. It doesn't matter if it's big or small, the important thing is that it's a place that helps you give your best. Spend time and care designing it, because this is where you will build the life you've always dreamed of. When your office is in harmony with you, working from home stops being an obligation and becomes an experience you enjoy every day.

Successful Habits for Working from Home

Working from home can be an incredibly rewarding experience, but it also has its challenges. One of the biggest is maintaining a consistent level of productivity and motivation. Without the traditional structures of an office, such as fixed schedules, supervisors, and colleagues around, it's easy to fall into procrastination or feel disconnected. That's why developing successful habits is essential to achieving your goals and enjoying this lifestyle.

The first key habit is to establish a daily routine. Even if you're at home, you need a clear schedule for starting and ending your workday. Waking up at the same time every day, dressing as if you were going out, and planning your tasks are all steps that help you get into work mode. You don't have to wear formal clothes, but avoiding staying in your pajamas makes a big difference in your attitude. A stable routine gives you structure and prevents you from wasting time deciding what to do next.

Another important habit is to organize your day before you start. Take a few minutes, either the night before or first thing in the morning, to make a list of the tasks you need to complete. Prioritize them and focus on the most important ones first. This prevents you from feeling overwhelmed and helps you stay focused. Plus, checking tasks off your list will give you a sense of accomplishment that will motivate you to keep going.

Setting boundaries is essential when working from home. Often, friends, family, or roommates may think that because you're home, you're available to chat or run errands. Learn to say no and communicate your work schedule clearly. Creating a dedicated physical space to work also helps. When you're at your desk, it's your work zone, and when you leave it, you can relax. These boundaries aren't just for others, they're for you too. Respect your own schedule and avoid working outside of the hours you've set for yourself.

The next habit is all about taking care of your physical well-being. When you work from home, it's easy to spend hours sitting in front of a screen without realizing you haven't moved. Schedule regular breaks to stretch, walk around, or just rest your eyes.

Not only does this help you feel better physically, but it also improves your concentration. Also make sure you eat healthy and stay hydrated. Avoiding constant snacking and opting for balanced meals will keep your energy stable throughout the day.

Time management is another key pillar. Working from home gives you a lot of freedom, but that also means you need to be disciplined. Use techniques like the Pomodoro method, where you work for 25 minutes focused on a task and then take a short break. These strategies help you stay productive without burning out. Also avoid common distractions, like social media or TV, during your work hours. If you need to, use tools or apps that temporarily block distracting websites.

One habit that many people overlook is making time for continuous learning. Working from home gives you the flexibility to invest in your personal and professional development. You can take online courses, read books related to your field, or learn new skills that help you diversify your income. Doing this not only makes you more competent, but it also keeps your mind active and motivated.

Staying connected with other people is another crucial habit. Working from home can be lonely if you don’t make an effort to connect with colleagues, friends, or even other people who are also working remotely. Participate in online communities, attend virtual meetings, or simply organize regular calls with your professional contacts. These interactions help you stay inspired and give you new perspectives to tackle challenges.

Finally, one of the most important habits is to celebrate your achievements. When you work from home, it's easy to forget to acknowledge your own successes because you don't have a boss or colleagues to do it for you. Take time to reflect on what you've accomplished at the end of each day or week. Acknowledging your progress, no matter how small, gives you the motivation to keep going.

Developing these habits doesn’t happen overnight. It takes practice, adjustment, and commitment. But once you integrate them into your life, working from home becomes a more productive, balanced, and fulfilling experience. These habits not only improve your work performance, but they also help you build a life you fully enjoy. Working from home isn't just a way to make a living—it's an opportunity to design your own success.

The Comfort Zone Trap

The comfort zone trap is one of the biggest obstacles you'll face when working from home. It's that feeling of security that comes from doing what you already know, from keeping things easy and comfortable. At first, it seems like a positive thing. After all, who doesn't want to feel safe and relaxed? But here's the problem: the comfort zone doesn't lead to growth, and when you get stuck in it, you stagnate.

When you work from home, it's very easy to fall into this trap. You have your space, your routines, and no one is directly pressuring you to do more. However, if you get too comfortable, you start to limit your potential. Maybe you decide not to learn that new skill because you think you don't need it right now. Or maybe you stick with the same clients or projects because changing seems complicated. At first it seems like a logical decision, but over time, you realize you're missing out on opportunities.

The comfort zone isn't just a physical place, it's also a mental one. It's when you tell yourself things like "this is fine for now," "I don't need to try as hard," or "this is enough for me." While those phrases seem harmless, they're actually barriers that keep you from moving forward. Working from home gives you the freedom to control your life, but it also puts you in a position where you're responsible for pushing yourself forward. No one else will do it for you.

Getting out of your comfort zone isn't easy, but it's necessary. The first step is to recognize that you're in it. Ask yourself if the decisions you're making are out of convenience or out of genuine interest in moving forward. If you're choosing the easy option all the time, it's a sign that you need a change. Once you recognize that, start taking small steps into the unknown. You don't need to do something huge right away, but you do need to move in the right direction.

For example, if you feel like you've mastered your current job, try learning something new that will give you more tools. If you're afraid to pursue bigger or different clients, start by researching what they need and how you might be able to help them. If you're having trouble breaking out of your routine, change something small, like working in a different location or rearranging your schedule. The important thing is to constantly challenge yourself, even in small ways. Each time you do, you expand your comfort zone and become a stronger, more capable version of yourself.

Another important aspect of getting out of your comfort zone is accepting failure as part of the process. When you do something new, it's not always going to turn out right. But this isn't a bad thing. In fact, mistakes are one of the best ways to learn. Every time you fail, you're one step closer to finding the right way to do it. Working from home gives you the space to experiment without the pressure of a boss or an office environment, so use that to your advantage.

One trick to avoid falling into the comfort zone trap is to surround yourself with people who inspire you. Look for others who are working from home and achieving amazing things. Talking to them, hearing their stories, and learning from their experiences can motivate you to try something new. You can also read books, listen to podcasts, or follow people who push you to get out of your routine. The energy of others is contagious, and surrounding yourself with people who think big will help you do so too.

Finally, remember that your comfort zone isn't a place you should avoid altogether. Sometimes, you need a break, and it's okay to enjoy the peace of mind it offers. But you can't stay there for too long. Life is about growth, and growth always happens outside of that zone. Every time you dare to step out of it, you're getting closer to your goals and the life you truly want.

The comfort zone trap is comfortable, but it’s also dangerous. It steals your time, your opportunities, and often your dreams. If you choose to do nothing, days, months, and years will pass, and you’ll find yourself in the same place, wondering what could have been. Instead, if you dare to go out, even a little each day, you’ll discover a world full of possibilities. Working from home is the perfect opportunity to design your life, but to do so, you need to overcome that comfort and venture into the unknown. That's where the magic really begins.

The Patience of Success from Home

The patience of home-based success is one of the most important lessons you need to learn if you want to build a life working for yourself. When you first start working from home, it can be easy to imagine that success will come quickly. Maybe you think that in a few weeks you'll have a steady stream of income or that everything will fall into place right away. However, the reality is that success, especially when you work from home, takes time, effort, and most of all, patience.

At first, things may not go as you expected. Maybe you struggle to find clients, you feel lost organizing your day, or your income isn't as high as you imagined. This is a crucial moment, because many people, not seeing quick results, become demotivated and give up. But this is where patience plays a fundamental role. Understanding that great achievements take time will help you get through this initial stage.

When you work from home, you are building something from scratch. It can be a business, a freelance career, or any other way to generate income. This is not like a traditional job where you receive a fixed salary at the end of the month. Here, the results directly depend on your effort and the strategies you implement. And like everything worthwhile in life, this process takes time. It's like planting a seed. At first, you don't see anything. You have to water it, take care of it, and wait. But with patience, that seed grows into a strong and productive tree.

Patience also involves learning to handle uncertainty. When you work from home, you don't always know exactly when the results will come. Maybe one month is great, and the next you face some challenges. This is completely normal. Instead of getting discouraged, use these moments to learn and adjust your approach. Every challenge is an opportunity to grow and improve, but you need patience to see the lessons amidst the difficulties.

Another important aspect of patience is to avoid comparing yourself to others. It's easy to look at someone else working from home and think they have it all figured out. Maybe they seem to make more money or be more successful, but what you don't see is all the work and years it probably took them to get there. Every person has their own path and their own pace. Comparing yourself to others will only make you feel frustrated and divert your attention from what really matters: your personal progress.

Being patient also means celebrating the small achievements. Often, we are so focused on reaching our big goals that we forget to acknowledge the small wins along the way. Maybe you landed your first client, learned a new skill, or simply became more organized with your time. These things, even though they may seem small, are important steps toward success. Acknowledging them not only motivates you, but it also reminds you that you are moving forward.

Patience is not passivity. It's not about sitting around waiting for things to happen on their own. It's about continuing to work, learn, and push yourself, even when results don't come as quickly as you'd like. It's about trusting that if you do the right thing and stay focused, success will eventually come. It's a balance between action and waiting, between perseverance and calm.

To develop patience, it's helpful to set realistic expectations. If you expect immediate results, you're more likely to get frustrated. Instead, understand that this is a long-term process. Create short-, medium-, and long-term goals, and work toward them little by little. Having a clear plan will help you stay focused and remember that every step counts, even if it seems small at the moment.

It's also important to take care of your emotional well-being during this process. Patience can be difficult when you're feeling anxious or pressured. Practicing activities like meditation, exercise, or simply taking a break when you need it can help you stay calm. When you're emotionally balanced, it's easier to be patient and face challenges with a positive attitude.

Remember that working from home is an amazing opportunity, but it is also a responsibility. You are the master of your time and your success. Patience not only helps you endure the hardships, but it also allows you to enjoy the journey. Because that is what really matters: not only achieving your goals, but also growing and learning in the process.

The patience of working from home is like a muscle that you must train. It doesn't develop overnight, but with practice and determination, it becomes one of your greatest strengths. In the end, you'll realize that all the effort was worth it. Working from home isn't just a way to make a living, it's a path to a freer, more meaningful life that's more aligned with your dreams. And to get there, patience will be your best ally.

Key to Success

The key to success when working from home isn't some magic secret or special talent reserved for only a select few. It's the result of a combination of factors that, when applied consistently, lead to impressive results. The best part is that anyone can learn and put them into practice, as long as they're willing to commit to the process.

The first element of this key is discipline. Working from home may seem like an ideal idea, but it also has its challenges. Without the structure of a traditional office, you are the one who defines your schedule, your goals, and your pace. This can be liberating, but it can also become a problem if you don’t have discipline. It means getting up on time, working the necessary hours, and resisting distractions. The temptation to put off tasks or waste time surfing the internet is always there, but discipline helps you stay focused on what matters.

Another essential component is planning. Success doesn't just happen; it's the result of good organization. Before you start your day, take a few minutes to plan your day. Make a list of priority tasks and set clear goals. This not only helps you stay focused, but it also gives you a sense of purpose. When you know exactly what you have to do, it's easier to move forward with confidence and without wasting time on unnecessary decisions.

The ability to adapt is another crucial factor. Working from home means an ever-changing environment. You may have a lot of work one day and hardly any the next. A strategy that worked in the past may no longer be effective. The key is to stay flexible and be willing to try new things. Learn to view changes as opportunities for improvement, not obstacles. Adaptability will allow you to keep moving forward even when things don't go the way you expected.

Perseverance is a must. Success from home doesn't happen overnight. There will be good days and tough days, times when everything seems to be going against you. But this is where many people fall behind: they give up too soon. Perseverance means keeping going even when the results aren't immediate. It's having the patience to wait and the courage to try again and again. If you keep working, learning, and adjusting your approach, eventually the results will come.

Another key ingredient to success is a constant learning mindset. The world is constantly evolving, and working from home is no exception. Tools, trends, and strategies change, and you need to be willing to continually learn and improve. This can mean taking courses, reading books, attending seminars, or simply spending time researching and experimenting. The more you learn, the more prepared you will be to face challenges and take advantage of opportunities.

Time management is equally important. When you work from home, time is your most valuable resource. Learning to manage it properly can make the difference between success and failure. This means identifying your most productive hours and spending that time on your most important tasks. It also involves learning to say no to things that don't contribute to your goals, such as unnecessary meetings or social engagements that interfere with your work.

Self-confidence is also a key piece. Working from home can be lonely, and you may sometimes doubt your abilities or decisions. However, it's important to remember that success starts in your mind. Trust that you have what it takes to succeed and that every step you take, no matter how small, brings you closer to your goals. Confidence doesn't mean you'll never fail, but that you'll know how to get back up every time you do.

Finally, balance is key. Working from home can make it easy for work and personal life to blend together, which can lead to burnout. It's important to set clear boundaries and set aside time for yourself and the people you love. Success isn't just about making money, it's also about enjoying the life you're creating.

In short, the key to success from home is not one single element, but a combination of discipline, planning, adaptability, perseverance, constant learning, time management, self-confidence, and balance. If you commit to applying these principles, you will be building a solid foundation to achieve your goals. And the most exciting thing is that every day is a new opportunity to improve, grow, and get closer to the life you truly want. The road will not always be easy, but it will certainly be worth it.

The Power of Digital Marketing

The power of digital marketing is something you can't ignore if you want to be successful working from home. It's a powerful tool that allows you to reach thousands, even millions of people, without ever leaving your workplace. In the past, promoting a product or service required huge investments in print, TV or radio ads. Today, thanks to the internet, anyone with a connected device can showcase their offering to the entire world, and that's a game-changer.

Digital marketing is all about leveraging platforms like social media, search engines, email, and websites to connect with your audience. The first thing you need to understand is that it's not just about selling, it's about building relationships. People don't buy products or services, they buy solutions to their problems, and that's what you need to offer. When using digital marketing, your main goal should be to show how what you offer can improve people's lives.

One of the most fascinating aspects of digital marketing is segmentation. Instead of spending money trying to reach everyone, you can focus your efforts on people who are actually interested in what you do. For example, if you work from home offering consulting, you can target your ads to people who are looking for specific solutions in your area. Not only does this increase your chances of success, but it also makes your investment more efficient.

To get started with digital marketing, the first thing you need is a solid online presence. This includes having a professional website and active social media profiles relevant to your audience. Think of your website as your digital home, a place where people can get to know you, understand what you do, and most importantly, trust you. Make sure your site is easy to navigate, has clear information, and if possible, includes testimonials or success stories that support what you offer.

Social media is another key digital marketing tool. Platforms like Facebook, Instagram, LinkedIn, and TikTok have millions of active users daily, which means your audience is out there. But not all social media is created equal, and you don't need to be on all of them. It's best to choose one or two platforms that are most relevant to your target audience and focus on creating valuable, consistent content. Post tips, stories, interesting facts, or anything that will connect with your audience and demonstrate your expertise.

Content is the heart of digital marketing. When you create useful, informative, or entertaining content, you naturally attract people's attention. This can include blog articles, videos, podcasts, or even simple social media posts. The key is to be authentic and offer value. Think about the questions your audience might have and answer those questions through your content. This not only positions you as an expert, but it also builds trust.

Email marketing is another strategy that you shouldn't overlook. Despite being one of the oldest tools in digital marketing, it's still incredibly effective. An email list allows you to communicate directly with people who are interested in what you do. You can send them updates, special offers, tips, or any other information that would be useful to them. Best of all, you have full control over this list, unlike social media, where algorithms can limit who sees your posts.

Digital marketing also includes the use of paid ads. Tools like Google Ads or social media ads allow you to promote your business at a relatively low cost. The best thing about digital ads is that you can measure their effectiveness in real time. You know exactly how many people clicked on your ad, visited your site, or purchased your product. This allows you to fine-tune your strategies and make sure you're spending your money wisely.

However, digital marketing isn’t all about tools and strategies. It’s also about understanding people. Get to know your audience. Listen to their needs, their problems, and their desires. Answer their questions and genuinely care about helping them. When people feel like you care about them, they’re more likely to trust you and eventually buy what you offer.

Another crucial aspect of digital marketing is consistency. Don’t expect results overnight. Building an online presence and a loyal audience takes time. You may post for weeks or months before you see significant results. But if you stay consistent, creating quality content and connecting with your audience, the results will come.

Finally, don't be afraid to experiment. Digital marketing is constantly evolving, and what works today may not work tomorrow. Try different strategies, measure your results, and adjust as needed. Flexibility is one of the biggest advantages of this form of marketing, and you should take full advantage of it.

The power of digital marketing is immense, but it requires commitment, creativity, and patience. If you do it right, it can be the bridge that connects your home-based business to success. It's a tool that allows you to compete with big companies and reach people who truly value what you offer, all from the comfort of your own home.

Build a Business with Passive Income

Building a passive income business is one of the best ways to make money from home and achieve financial freedom. But what does passive income really mean? Essentially, it's creating systems or products that generate consistent income with little to no ongoing effort on your part. This doesn't mean you don't have to work. In the beginning, building this type of business takes time, effort, and a lot of dedication. However, once you've established it, the work required to maintain it can be minimal, allowing you to enjoy your time while the money keeps coming in.

The first step to building a passive income business is to identify something that can work without you having to be present all the time. For example, digital products like eBooks, online courses, or music are great options. Once you create a book or course, you can sell it over and over again without having to re-create it. Similarly, if you have creative skills, you could design templates, illustrations, or downloadable content and sell it on specific platforms.

Another example is affiliate platforms. If you have a blog, YouTube channel, or social media page with a sizable audience, you can recommend products or services and earn a commission for each sale made through your links. This works especially well if you focus on a niche where you have experience and can build trust with your followers.

Passive income can also come from physical goods, although they usually require a bit more initial investment. For example, if you have space, you could rent out rooms through online platforms or even invest in long-term rental properties. In this case, although there is some upkeep associated with it, the income you can generate over the long term justifies the effort.

A common strategy in the world of passive income is to invest in stocks or funds that pay dividends. Here, instead of building a product or service, you put your money to work for you. Over time, the profits from your investments can become a steady stream of income that supplements what you earn from other activities. However, this option requires good financial planning and patience to let your investments grow.

It's important to remember that while passive income may sound like the perfect solution, building it isn't something that happens overnight. You need a long-term mindset. Success in this type of business comes with consistency, planning, and a willingness to learn. In the beginning, you'll likely have to invest hours developing your product, creating content, or learning how to promote it. But if you do a good job, those initial efforts will multiply over time.

In addition to building a product or service, marketing plays a vital role in passive income. It's not enough to just have something good, you also need to make sure the right people find it. That's why it's important to learn how to use tools like social media ads, search engine optimization, and email marketing. Not only will these strategies bring in customers, but they can also be automated so they work even while you're sleeping.

A great advantage of passive income is that it allows you to diversify your income streams. You don't need to limit yourself to just one idea. For example, you can have an online course, affiliate products on your blog, and a rental property at the same time. This way, if one source has a bad month, the others can balance out your earnings. Diversification is key to long-term financial stability and peace of mind.

It's also crucial to manage your expectations. Sometimes passive income isn't completely passive. There are times when you'll need to revise, update, or improve your system. For example, if you created an online course, you may need to add new content to keep it relevant. If you have a blog, you'll likely need to keep publishing content to attract traffic. This doesn't mean the system doesn't work, it's just part of the process.

Finally, building a passive income business requires a clear vision of what you want to accomplish. Ask yourself why you are doing this. Do you want more time for your family? Do you want to travel without financial worries? Or do you simply want the peace of mind that comes from knowing your financial future is secure?

Having a clear purpose will help you stay focused and motivated, even when you encounter challenges along the way.

Building a passive income business is an investment in your future. It's the way to break free from the idea of trading your time for money and start creating a life where money works for you. It's not an easy road, but it's one filled with opportunity and reward. With patience, dedication, and a solid strategy, you can build a business that not only generates consistent income, but also allows you to live the life you've always dreamed of.

Monetize Your Talents and Passions

Monetizing your talents and passions is one of the most rewarding ways to make money from home. Not only does it allow you to generate income, but it also gives you the opportunity to work on something you truly enjoy and find fulfilling. The idea of turning what you love into your source of income may seem like a dream, but with focus and a clear strategy, it is completely possible.

The first step is to identify your talents and passions. Ask yourself what you like to do and what you're good at. It could be something as creative as painting, writing, or cooking, or something more technical like solving math problems, programming, or repairing objects. Maybe you have specialized knowledge in an area that other people value, or you're good at listening and giving advice. All of these have the potential to become a source of income if you know how to present them to the world.

Once you're clear on what your talent or passion is, it's important to consider how you can solve a problem or fulfill a need with it. People are willing to pay for things that make their lives easier, teach them something new, or provide entertainment. For example, if you love cooking, you could create recipe videos, offer online cooking classes, or even write a recipe book. If you love graphic design, you could offer logo creation services or sell your designs as downloadable products.

The key to monetizing your talents is to offer something unique. It's not just about doing what you love, but doing it in a way that stands out. For example, if you're passionate about photography, think about how you can differentiate yourself. Maybe you could specialize in product photography for online stores or images for social media. If you love writing, you could focus on creating engaging content for blogs or writing personalized stories for special occasions. Originality is what will make people choose you over other options.

Another important aspect is learning to value your work. Often, when we like something, we tend to undervalue it or think that it is not good enough to charge for. This couldn't be further from the truth.

If something has value to you and you can prove that it has value to others, it deserves a fair price. Research how much other people are charging for similar services or products and set a price that reflects the quality and effort you put into your work.

Online platforms are a powerful ally to monetize your talents and passions. Sites like Etsy, Fiverr, YouTube, Patreon, or social media like Instagram and TikTok allow you to reach a wide audience with specific interests. For example, if you are passionate about making crafts, Etsy can be a great platform to sell your products. If you love teaching, YouTube or TikTok can be the perfect place to share tutorials and attract followers who could later become customers.

Consistency is key. Monetizing your talents isn't something that happens overnight. It takes time to build an audience, gain their trust, and prove the value of what you offer. Post content regularly, engage with your audience, and listen to their feedback. Not only will this help you improve, but it will also strengthen the connection you have with people interested in your work.

Another effective way to monetize your passions is through collaborations. Find people or brands that share similar interests and propose working together on mutually beneficial projects. For example, if you are a fitness enthusiast and have a social media account, you could collaborate with brands that sell sportswear or health products. These partnerships can open doors and increase your reach, while allowing you to continue doing what you love.

It's important not to get discouraged if the results aren't immediate. Monetizing a talent or passion often requires experimenting with different approaches. Maybe your first idea doesn't work out the way you hoped, but that doesn't mean you should give up. Learn from each attempt and adjust your strategy. Flexibility and a willingness to adapt are key to finding the right path.

Finally, remember that monetizing your talents and passions doesn’t mean you have to lose the love for what you do. Keep a balance between working to generate income and enjoying the creative process or the act of sharing your knowledge. If something starts to feel like a burden, take a break, reevaluate your goals, and remember why you started in the first place.

Monetizing your talents and passions is an incredible opportunity to live a more fulfilling and authentic life. It allows you to combine your skills with your interests and build a business that reflects who you truly are. It may not be an easy path, but with dedication, patience, and an open mindset, you can achieve it. The best part is that by doing so, you will not only be making money, but also living a life of purpose and passion.

Family and Work Under One Roof

Working from home while sharing the same space with your family can be a wonderful experience, but it also presents unique challenges that you must learn to manage. The idea of having your loved ones nearby while you work is lovely, but to make it work, you need to set clear boundaries, get organized, and learn to balance your work and family responsibilities effectively. This chapter is dedicated to exploring how to achieve this without sacrificing the quality of time you spend with your family or productivity at work.

The first thing you need to understand is that working from home doesn't mean being available for everything at all times. It's easy to fall into the trap of trying to tackle family tasks while you're in the middle of your work obligations. That's why it's crucial to set clear schedules. Define specific blocks of time for work and make sure everyone at home respects them. For example, if you decide you'll work from 9 to 2, communicate this to your family and organize your space in a way that minimizes distractions.

Your workspace also plays an important role. If possible, create an area dedicated solely to your work. This can be a separate room, a corner in the living room, or even a desk in your bedroom. The important thing is that it is a place where you can concentrate and that both you and your family understand that when you are there, you are working. This will not only help you focus, but it will also send a clear signal to others that you should not be interrupted, except in an emergency.

Communication with your family is key. Talk openly with them about your work responsibilities and the importance of maintaining a balance. If you have young children, explain to them in simple words that even though you are at home, there are times when you need to focus. You can use visual cues like a sign on the door of your workspace or an object that indicates you are in "work mode." This will help them understand when it is the right time to come over.

On the other hand, it is also important to be flexible and find moments to connect with your family during the day. One of the advantages of working from home is that you have the opportunity to be present in the daily lives of your loved ones. Take advantage of breaks to share a coffee with your partner, play a few minutes with your children or enjoy a meal together. These small moments can strengthen your relationships and make everyone appreciate your presence at home more.

If you share a space with children, keep in mind that they have their own needs and routines, too. Planning activities that they can do independently while you work can be a big help. Coloring books, board games, or even online learning sessions can keep them busy while you get things done. Plus, involving them in certain household chores or teaching them about your job can be an enriching experience for both them and you.

The balance between family and work isn't always perfect, and there will be days when you feel like you can't get it all done. During those times, it's important to be compassionate with yourself. Remember that you're doing the best you can in a situation that isn't always easy. Don't be afraid to ask for help if you need it. Sometimes, delegating certain responsibilities, whether at work or at home, can make a big difference.

Another effective strategy is to plan family activities after work as a way to unwind and reward yourself for a productive day. Maybe you can watch a movie together, cook a special dinner, or just go for a walk. Not only will this help you relax, but it will also strengthen your bond with your loved ones.

However, it's also important to set aside time for yourself. Working from home and being surrounded by your family all the time can be overwhelming if you don't have moments of privacy. Whether it's reading a book, meditating, exercising, or just sitting in silence, make sure to include personal time in your daily routine. This will help you stay balanced and have the energy to tackle your responsibilities.

Finally, it's important to recognize that working from home with your family is a continuous learning process. There will be times when everything flows perfectly and other times when it feels like chaos. The important thing is to not give up. With patience, organization, and constant communication, you can find a system that works for everyone.

Sharing a roof with your family while working is an experience that can strengthen family ties if handled appropriately. It gives you the opportunity to be an active part of their lives while pursuing your work goals. With the necessary adjustments, you can turn this lifestyle into one filled with harmony, productivity, and happiness.

Disconnect to Reconnect

Disconnecting to reconnect is a fundamental concept for those who work from home. With so many responsibilities and constant connection to electronic devices, it is easy to feel overwhelmed and disconnected from what really matters. While working from home may seem like a dream come true, it can also become an endless cycle of work if you don’t set clear boundaries. In this chapter, we will explore why disconnecting is essential and how to do it effectively to recharge, strengthen your relationships, and improve your quality of life.

When you work from home, the lines between your work life and your personal life can become blurred. The temptation to check emails, take calls, or finish projects outside of work hours is great, but this practice can drain your physical and mental energy. That's why learning to disconnect from work at the end of the day isn't a luxury—it's a necessity. By turning off your computer and putting away your work tools, you're giving your mind and body the signal that it's time to rest and recharge.

Unplugging doesn't just mean stepping away from work, it also means cutting down on screen time. Social media, email, and messaging apps can keep you in a constant state of alert. This can affect your ability to relax and enjoy the present moment. Try setting specific times to use your devices, and outside of that time, unplug them or put them on silent. This will allow you to focus on activities that truly fulfill you, like reading, exercising, or spending time with loved ones.

One of the best ways to unwind is to get out of the house. While working from home offers convenience, it can also lead to spending too much time in the same environment. This can lead to monotony and take a toll on your mental health. Go for a walk, go to the park, exercise outdoors, or simply explore your neighborhood. A change of scenery can help you clear your mind and gain a fresh perspective. Plus, spending time in nature has proven benefits for reducing stress and improving your mood.

Unplugging also gives you the opportunity to reconnect with the people who are important to you. When you're constantly focused on work or your devices, you can miss out on valuable moments with your family and friends. Make time for yourself exclusively with your loved ones. It can be something as simple as sharing a meal without phones on the table, having a heart-to-heart conversation, or enjoying an activity together. Not only will these moments strengthen your relationships, they'll also remind you why you're working so hard.

Reconnecting doesn't just involve others, it also means reconnecting with yourself. When you disconnect, you have the opportunity to reflect on your goals, your achievements, and your dreams. It's a time to ask yourself if you're on the right path or if you need to make adjustments. You can use this time to practice meditation, journal, or simply sit quietly and listen to your thoughts. These practices can help you find clarity and purpose, which in turn will improve your focus when you return to work.

It's important to remember that unplugging isn't something you should do only when you're feeling burned out. Make it part of your daily or weekly routine. Maybe you can set a specific time each night to step away from screens, or dedicate a full day each week to completely disconnecting from work. Consider this an investment in your long-term well-being. The more you take care of yourself, the more energy and focus you'll have to tackle your responsibilities.

A key aspect of successfully unplugging is not feeling guilty about doing so. In our culture, we often associate productivity with being busy all the time, but this approach isn't sustainable. Resting and recharging doesn't mean you're being lazy—it means you're prioritizing your health and your ability to perform at your best. Learn to give yourself permission to unplug without regret, knowing that this time is essential to your long-term success.

In conclusion, disconnecting to reconnect is an essential skill in today's world, especially for those working from home. It allows you to set healthy boundaries, recharge your energies, strengthen your relationships, and rediscover what really matters. By doing so, you will not only improve your personal well-being, but you will also be more productive and efficient at work. Remember that disconnecting is not an obstacle to your success, it is a fundamental part of it.

Breaking the Myth of Isolation

One of the most common fears when it comes to working from home is the idea of isolation. Many people believe that not being surrounded by colleagues in an office or interacting with others in a work environment will make them feel lonely, disconnected from the world, or even depressed. While this fear may have some foundation if no action is taken, it is entirely possible to work from home without falling into social isolation. In this chapter, we're going to explore how to break this myth and ensure that working from home is a balanced and enriching experience.

It’s true that working from home can reduce the amount of spontaneous social interactions you used to have in an office, such as chats at the coffee machine or casual meetings. However, this doesn’t mean you have to live in a bubble. Isolation doesn’t happen because you work from home, but because you don’t take steps to maintain and build relationships. The key is to be proactive. Don’t wait for social connections to happen on their own, make them part of your everyday life.

One of the most effective ways to break the isolation myth is to establish a social routine. This can include scheduling video calls with friends, participating in online groups related to your work or interests, or even attending virtual events or workshops. While digital interactions don't always replace in-person ones, they are a great way to stay connected to the world and share ideas with others who have similar interests to you.

Also, don't underestimate the power of local connections. Working from home doesn't mean you have to be tied to your desk all the time. Make time to get out and participate in activities in your community. This could be a weekly coffee with friends, joining a yoga class at a nearby center, or simply taking a walk in the park and chatting with the people you meet. These small interactions can make a big difference in your perception of connection with others.

If you have colleagues or clients that you work with regularly, make an effort to maintain consistent, meaningful communication with them. Don't limit conversations to strictly work-related topics. Take a moment to ask how they're doing, take an interest in their lives, or share something about yourself. This kind of personal connection can help you feel like part of a team, even if you're all working from different locations.

Another helpful strategy is to look for coworking spaces in your area. Even though you work from home, nothing prevents you from spending one or two days a week in a place where you can interact with other professionals. These spaces are often designed to encourage collaboration and interaction, which can help you break away from routine and find new perspectives.

Breaking the isolation myth also requires you to acknowledge and manage your emotions. It's normal that at times you may feel lonely or disconnected. Instead of ignoring those feelings, use those emotions as a signal to take action. Maybe it's time to call a friend, take a social break, or even consider changing your routine to include more social activities.

If you have family at home, don't forget to include them in your day in a balanced way. Even though you're working, it's important to take advantage of the moments when you can interact with them. Sharing a meal, chatting during a break, or simply being present for some quality time can help you feel more connected and less isolated.

Finally, remember that isolation isn't unique to working from home. Many people who work in offices can also feel lonely or disconnected. The difference is in how you choose to handle your situation. By taking conscious steps to maintain your social relationships and establishing a balanced routine, you can break the isolation myth and enjoy the benefits of working from home without feeling lonely.

In short, isolation doesn't have to be an inevitable consequence of working from home. With planning, action, and a little creativity, you can build a rich and fulfilling social life that complements your remote work style. Working from home gives you the freedom to make your own rules and find a balance that works for you, both professionally and personally. Don't let the fear of isolation stop you from enjoying this lifestyle. Instead, use it as an opportunity to rediscover the importance of human connections and strengthen your relationships, both in and out of the workplace.

The Life You Always Dreamed Of

The life you've always dreamed of is not an abstract concept or an unattainable ideal. It's a goal you can build day by day, step by step, if you're clear about what you really want and are willing to work for it. For many, working from home represents that dream: freedom of time, the ability to organize your days according to your priorities and, most importantly, absolute control over how you live your life. But to get there, it's essential to understand what that dream life means to you and how to transform it into a tangible reality.

Imagine waking up every morning without the sound of an annoying alarm clock, without the stress of rushing to beat traffic or get to an office on time. Instead, you have the luxury of starting your day at your own pace. Maybe you want to spend the first hour having a quiet breakfast with your family, going for a relaxing walk, or reading a book that inspires you. Working from home allows you to design a schedule that not only suits your work needs, but also your personal well-being and relationships.

The dream of living the way you really want doesn’t mean that everything will be perfect or easy. However, when you have the power to decide how you organize your time and energy, you can dedicate more space to the things that really matter. Maybe you always dreamed of learning a new language, spending more time with your children, or cultivating a hobby that you had put aside due to lack of time. Working from home not only gives you the freedom to dream, but also the opportunity to act on those dreams.

Living the life you've always wanted also means redefining success. For some people, success is making a lot of money. For others, it's having free time to enjoy it. What does success mean to you? Maybe it's having time to take your kids to school, cook a home-cooked meal, or just enjoy a leisurely day. Working from home gives you the opportunity to align your professional goals with your personal values, something few people achieve in a traditional work environment.

An important part of living the life you want is having a work-life balance. When you work from home, this balance can be difficult at first, as it's easy to blend the two worlds. But with discipline and planning, you can find a system that works for you. The key is to set clear boundaries. Have a defined space to work, a set schedule, and time dedicated solely to your family, friends, and of course, yourself.

Often, the dream of many people is not just to live comfortably, but also to find purpose in what they do. Working from home is not just about avoiding traffic or wearing comfortable clothes. It is about building a career or business that is aligned with your passions and skills. This is the time to ask yourself what truly makes you happy and how you can turn it into a source of income. When you love what you do, even the tough days feel more bearable, because you know you are working on something that truly matters to you.

You can't talk about the dream life without mentioning financial freedom. Earning money from home gives you the opportunity to break away from the constraints of a fixed salary. Although it can be challenging to establish a stable income at first, once you do, you have the possibility to scale your earnings and plan your future more flexibly. You can save for travel, invest in your personal projects, or simply enjoy a life without immediate financial worries.

Another crucial aspect of life that you always dreamed of is having time for yourself. Many people spend most of their lives working for others, without making time for their own interests or self-care. Working from home allows you to prioritize activities like exercising, practicing meditation, or simply resting when you need it. This flexibility not only improves your physical and mental health, but also helps you be more productive and creative at work.

Living the life you always dreamed of also means connecting with the people you love. By not being limited by a strict schedule or physical location, you can spend more quality time with your family and friends. Maybe it's having dinner together every night, attending important events, or just being present for the everyday moments that really matter. These are the things that at the end of life you remember and value, and working from home can give you the opportunity to be there for them.

Ultimately, the life you've always dreamed of isn't something you achieve overnight. It's a journey filled with conscious decisions, small steps, and continuous adjustments. There will be days when you feel challenged, but those moments are also opportunities to grow and reaffirm why you chose this path. Every day you spend building this life is a victory, and every effort is worth it when you start to see how your reality aligns with your dreams.

In conclusion, living the life you always dreamed of is more than a fantasy. It is a real possibility if you are willing to take the leap, commit to your goals, and maintain the discipline necessary to make them a reality. Working from home is a powerful tool that can help you achieve that vision, but real change begins with you. Define what a dream life means to you, take action, and don’t stop until you are living each day with purpose, joy, and freedom.

www.ingramcontent.com/pod-product-compliance
Lightning Source LLC
LaVergne TN
LVHW091121150826
845673LV00002B/915